Prescribed Burn

poems by

Sara Biel

Finishing Line Press
Georgetown, Kentucky

Prescribed Burn

Copyright © 2023 by Sara Biel
ISBN 979-8-88838-111-3 First Edition
All rights reserved under International and Pan-American Copyright Conventions. No part of this book may be reproduced in any manner whatsoever without written permission from the publisher, except in the case of brief quotations embodied in critical articles and reviews.

ACKNOWLEDGMENTS

"Telling;" "Spring;" "The Day After" and an earlier version of "Bean" first appeared in *Sparkle & Blink*
"Salt of Ourselves" first appeared in *HerWords*
"Warning" first appeared in *Words Upon the Waters* (Jukebox Press)
"Gravity's Daughter" will be included in *Button Eye Review* "Ghosts" anthology

I want to thank the friends and family who believed in and encouraged my writing. This book would have never come into being without the love and support of my daughters, Iris and Zoe and the encouragement of my spouse, Jay. I am particularly grateful for the guidance and support of Karla Brundage, MK Chavez, Colleen Shoshona McKee and Cassandra Dallett.

Publisher: Leah Huete de Maines
Editor: Christen Kincaid
Cover Art: *Natural Consequence* by David Russel Dawson
Author Photo: Rohan DaCosta PLAYDATEPHOTO on Instagram
Cover Design: Jay Trolinger

Order online: www.finishinglinepress.com
also available on amazon.com

Author inquiries and mail orders:
Finishing Line Press
PO Box 1626
Georgetown, Kentucky 40324
USA

Table of Contents

Defenestration 1

Heirloom 2

Archeology 3

I'm Still Here 4

Spring 5

Radio Silence 7

Prescribed Burn 9

How to Survive Quicksand 11

Losing our Language 13

Before 15

Illusion of Family 16

Telling 17

Awake 20

This Party Dress 21

Next Time 23

Inquisition 24

Sideways 25

The Salt of Ourselves 26

Conspirators 28

A Creek Song 29

The Day After 30

Bean 31

Winter Nest 32

Gravity's Daughter 33

Defenestration

Everyone needs a window.

Stepping from edge into flight
one brief freedom falls into the next
her face turns to kiss the concrete.

First, a glance in the direction of the street
nose presses against cool glass
she hears his voice droning, traffic staggering.

Her eyes shift
the possibilities become fewer
the lives farther between
a wet tongue slides across dry lips
a decision is made.

In one fluid movement
the window opens.
She knows only certainty
peace for a heart ground to dust.

There is no fear.

It must have been like swimming
on a hot sticky afternoon
a coolness waits
shifts below.

You know it is a gift meant for you.

Heirloom

The memory lies still
edgy and quiet
like trying to sleep
next to someone you don't want to touch.

We stood at the sink
watched freezing rain get caught in bare branches
deny the winter earth
the promise of spring.

The bruise
a brilliant betrayal
dragged her question from innocence
clung to the smooth porcelain
just above the soapy edge.

Words rolled clumsy from my lips
I softened them with sometimes.
That lifeline fell short
the wave pulled her in.

Our voices low
dropped sodden questions
into cloudy foam
their answers rose slick with shame.

We were the same
she told me
crying a duet into dishwater.

He is just like his father

Archeology

When I was young you were my moon
predictable cycles
of light and dark
crimson when too close
or dazzling in your frozen distance.

Our wordless connection
a sandcastle of hollow promises
crumbles in constant surf.

Every time
I begin again
unprepared
as disarmed as
every time.

Terrified
bones wait like broken windows.
Eyes catch like scissors.
Ears hold hollow regret.
Hands don't speak your language.
Mouth is swollen, disappointed.

I search the lines around your eyes
decipher the artifacts of your emotions.
With words scraped clean
only our tears run in tidal relation
a sputtering game of catch-up.

Words we never said flutter around us
confused as birds before a storm.

I'm Still Here
For my dad, Frank, 1927-1987

Long ago I would call
reach into the dark
wait for you
to lift me from muddy dreams
ground me in the lights of the city
there we counted
the cut glass tumbled sprawl
watched the sparkling emptiness
of night wind down.

We never talked about it.

Now
time tangles
twists
makes rubble of abandoned conversations.
I search for you in sleep.
Hope to catch you whistling in the moonlit house.
I struggle to remember what blue meant to the color of your eyes.

Our thinning thread vibrates
clear in the hum of midnight traffic.
This evening's mirror is an inkling
a shadow of our full selves.

I wonder
can you feel my small cool fist
a wish that bumps and tears
runs headlong into deep water.

You were
are still
my horizon

there

but never close.

Spring

Born at the water line
        mouth open, head tilted back.

A girl given a name
a cold hopeful season   an invisible ladder.

We watch her from the shore,
from striped chairs
buried in the dry warm sand.

She skips a small flat stone
        caught in laughing air
                tumbles, loses herself to the suck of the tide.

Go out
        comeback
                go   out
        come back

                go   out.

It's not like in the movies.
        She slips beneath the green horizon.
                Doesn't even wave.
Her mother calls.
We search the wind.

        Light
                shivers
                off ripples.
                I lift my words so their meaning surfaces

Exhale   inhale   call for help.

        The reflex,

        breath must be obeyed.

My explanation glassy   unfocused

        tongue cramps before it reaches the edge of my teeth.

Thoughts clot
    catch then flow from brackish pools.

                Like seeks like.
Rushes to join the inundation.

The warm waters swell   tap the degraded shoreline

wander into the   buzz of forgotten sun.

Words recede
      bob beyond
    her wrinkled reach.

Eyes close.
      Wind pushes sand over sand.
Her mind wades   rocks in the tick and sigh

    the hollow sound of anxious hands.

All my careful accounts   push her prayers sideways.

    They creep across our briny grief.
"Hush" she says.

                Drowning is silent.

Radio Silence

Birth-marked with complicity
my pale time peals
bearing the ordinary sharpness of morning.
Today, the radio suggests its own silence.

Here, in this place
hope becomes a corrupt beast
limps in circles
licks our hands.

This is California
home of sun and starlight
spangled in snowy oleander
poisonous beauty from
root to blossom.

Here two black men
found hanging
50 miles and 10 days apart.

Police suggest suicide.
Families say lynching.
We prefer not to hear.
We get distracted.

We choose the confusion of branches
fascinate on the color of leaves
roll the names of trees
against our teeth—
rather than hold the names of dead men
fluttering uneasily on our outstretched palms.

We look anywhere but here.

These deaths must not go unknown.
There were signs.
There are signs.

There have always been signs
at the library, near city hall,
in classrooms and convenience stores.

Centuries of looking away
head shaking, eyebrows an immune wrinkle.

We walk into fog
become its soft white blur.
Our dead-quiet
closes questions
with the decisive click of locked front doors.

Prescribed Burn

It began in a mix of soil and salt.
A fire set in my stillness.
I don't like to think about the windows shattered
the poison I pushed down stream.

Most of me came home.
Came awake.
Lips bruised in a crush of fear
skull sore from collisions and silent sobs.
Hair knotted and torn
messy convenience for his furious grip.
A handle to twist and drag
me stumbling, dumb
shuffled in disbelief from block to block.

That morning, miraculously alone
I slid into the stained bus seat.
Tears tucked in the tires' spin.
Breathed fully for the first time
in far too long.

My bitter tongue
swollen with unnamed crimes
dates, times, deceptions, dares
lines drawn and crossed
left choking on the curb.

Blood gathered
against my skin
stained all the places
his fingers gripped.

Blooming badges of dishonor.
I wrenched free.

Slipped his mother's ring
off my cold finger
couldn't watch as it bounced
in the rainy roadside gravel.

Sometimes
a door needs to slam
before it can close.

Sometimes
they burn fields so
something new might grow.

How to Survive Quicksand

Quicksand forms in saturated loose sand
when suddenly agitated.

I didn't know.
I didn't.
No.

I was made of sand
small granules clung together.
Grief as glue.

Oh, I knew.
There was always a space below the surface
something unsteady
built of last straws.

I have known
since the beginning
this cavernous place.

Born in silence
explored on hands and knees
understood with fingertips.

Do you know the topology of absence?
Have you read the guide for holding empty space?
Do you understand how to whisper promises to your pulse?
Sooth the corners where edges bare their teeth?

I didn't know.
I was once filled.
This was my home.

Silt washes down layers of doubt and disappointment.
Sand can weave a delicate structure
that will collapse in on itself
creating a vacuum
a dry sob when
there are no tears left.

I now know, exhaustion is the greatest risk.

There is a wetness seeping up from underground.

Now I know.
Breath without struggle
is the only way to float.

Losing our Language

I want to say something, I mean   do something.

                              pull her back in, the way
                the sound of a bell calls
                         children from a schoolyard or
                white cotton twine wraps
                              into a ball, drags a kite
                back through edgy wind.

She tells me there is something, she means   was something.

                              Now it hides like a pearl
                inside a prayer, the true
                                        need unnamed
                a leftover wish, loose
                                        and flying
                tucked behind my ear as I run
                              for the wheezing morning bus.

I try to remember something, no   to actually choose something.

                              To hold like a breath or the beam of
                  light from a half-closed door, a forgotten
                                    brightness so inviting shadows
              shake themselves and sulk
                                        in the corners, wash like cats.

She wants to explain something or maybe   just touch something.

                    The way temporary language sings in the wires
                    stretched between our cavernous hearts
                            the way our greetings are flocked in missing
                    and decorated with a weary cringe.

I need to break something but I mean   find something.

                            Look straight down the long hallway
              past every random cruelty and be
                        soothed by the way time can sway
              like a kelp forest, when we
                          notice only the golden flecks

floating   in   the   sun   warmed   sea.

Before

This morning I wake to your leaving
the dawn elbows night from the sky
the cry of a bird, a neighbor's alarm breaks
the viscous silence of the sleep-filled city.
Like a bubble popping
today begins.

Dawn stretches
its tide rises across the walls
fills the windows
patinas disheveled clouds.
Brief drizzle, in a nod of greeting
acknowledges

this is a day of parting.

My eyes accept morning
a sting at their corners.
A spasm at my core before
conscious surrender to the rightness of pain.
Grief is a testament to love.

The drizzle redoubles its effort
finger combs the early commute.
I hold these moments
the ones labeled before
an inhalation
tight with wishes and memories

knowing they must be released
with the sighs of the restless freeway.

Illusion of Family

These mornings I wake
my hands full of thorny dreams.
Grief clatters out of my hair
winks from every corner of this dust-filled room.

In the hard morning sunlight, my skin feels
out of place, remnants of memory
settle into our rumpled bed.

Our impasse rocks
waits patiently
for our exhausted return.

I do not need to trace these edges.
I'm well acquainted with the places my shadows accumulate.
The way I cut
and run at the infant hint of a lost game.
The way I tied so many knots around my fingers
I can no longer hold your hand.

Shame is blood-borne
pounds in my ears
sprawls in our contemptible rut.

Faith flies at half-mast.
Words cling to dead skin on the desert of my lips
crawl no farther.
Hopes flinch and evade my closed fist.
Come up for air in the moon's breathless shimmer.

They are trinkets.
They sink into our empty home.

They pacify like TV noise
lulls lonely people
with the illusion of family.

Telling

Winter sunset seeps crimson behind the mountains.
She cups her secret into my ear.
A match to my mother's
grief and anger pressed fingers to palm.
A string of stories.
Laundry on a line
wavering.

A tentative sovereignty born in blood.
Each story has a name:
Rita
Marguerite
Amy
Joan

My mother tells me her story
surrounded by snow
the early darkness of a northern night.
Our words hang on the phone line
cold and stiff.
"It should be easier. I want to see you after."

She told of driving with friends
Hollywood to Tijuana.
A girls' weekend, September of '63.
Smoking cigarettes
the top down-sun and wind.
A flask to pass around the car.
Someone knew someone who had a doctor's name.
It would be alright.

Later, in a dirty motel room
she cramped so hard she passed out
vomiting and bleeding through grey sheets.
She tried not to cry too loud, listened
to her friends dance in the courtyard bar outside the window
their laughter bleeding into scratchy radio music.
Her fear already scarring, curling into silence.

I listen to the squeaky crunch of tires in the snowy parking lot.
Dawn blinks out with the streetlights.
Almost strangers, our eyes roam the windshield
search for instructions in the ice left on the wipers.
Our teeth and hands
hold us carefully within our skins.
We are tangled
breathless in our unintended bonding
awkward in the intimacy of this accident.
Cloudy breath floats away from us.
In these strained moments time spreads
thin at its edges.

There was no guilt at this undoing.
He stamps his feet to keep warm.
Even in the orbit of his "honor"
I still live these hours alone.

In the room I pull away from him
but let him keep my hand.
Palm upturned, a place to put his thumb.
A way to feel effective.
I try not to squeeze too hard
in the clenching suck of being wrung out.

That afternoon
and through the whole slow husk of winter
we wander in a pantomime of coupled gestures.

Some secrets don't age, but calcify
breathe quietly, hands folded
lay claim with flat little smiles.

My secret,
natural as stretch marks.
Lingers,
mirrored in the eyes of older ladies.

Blooms with this telling
precarious and commonplace
A rose-colored morning from a storm-filled night.

Awake

I surface—
breach watery daze of dawn.
Nestle into a nest of weeds.
Thoughts scatter—
a pattern of white caps.
Silky traces of buried anchors.
Do these marks mean anything to you?
My heart falls open.
A vulnerable atlas,
archive of failure,
awash in ruminating waves.

I come unmoored—
wander the lacy vacancy
at the core of my bones.
Visit secrets I keep from myself
memories I banished before
they were breathed into being.
I float the endless looping hallways
my thoughts echo with
the distant sound of windows breaking.

I regret the time I've lost to this maze—
doubt a riptide
a legacy that leaves me
twisted
with too many words
and no wind to set them sail.

There are small moments
I come up for air
slapped awake by the view from
this damp shadow.

How long have I been dancing?

Whose blood stains my shoes?

This Party Dress

Chalk mountains
valleys frosted over
ash encrusted forests
bleached soil
cultivated by my indifferent gestures
my casually averted eyes

In this landscape
I am no guest
everyday life lived floating
propelled by pale buoyancy
privilege lives in my skin
pearls my voice, the slack of my walk
the way I hold my body
careless
immaculate
swaddled in anemic propriety

This riptide's silent seduction
phantom possessing every move
invisible to me as my breath
coils in my lungs
dusks every interaction in a hierarchy of fear
this genetic veil
this party dress
driven as snow
rings everything hollow

Wander through
minefield of my mind
I must embrace all discoveries
name them
tease out each curdled misconception
blooming in the fog
feeding amber waves
on oppression's nearest shore.

Too long I lived immune
rocked in the hush of "Normal"
insulated in the liquid aura of my whiteness
like water, blood runs to join its own
collects in deep places
gains the crest
voicing recent events in defense
rushes rough to smooth resistance

Blanched history preens
drones white noise
continues the echo
of inbred authority

I will not abide its
poison mythology
where fear eclipses fact
greed trumps community
ambition strangles compassion

Let's close the distance with humility
dare to speak
tear away silence
evoke level terrain
every word cast in equity cultivates
a land evolving toward integrity.

Next Time

Clouds crouch, warring cats between bunched mountains. The road, shadow slick, climbs in switches, dives, sways —dances lonely to the truck's exhausted growl. My thoughts stretch, a clothes-line hung with my mistakes. His anger pricks the tender cusp of my fear. He says he knows me, maybe better than I do. I stare past the mud-spattered windows, watch fickle greens and constant grays, the torn sky too cold for rain.

I find surprises in the bleak predictability of the late November highway. Half a naked bed frame, caught mid-tumble, clings to the rumpled slope. We pass a gas station, roof caved in, barren vines twist, reach out, broken windows caress the twilight. I curl against the door, cradle a vicious itch, regret refuses the satisfaction of my nails. I cool my bruised eye on the frozen window. Let my nose run onto my sleeve, reach for the grounding scent of laundry soap, the gentle flannel still holds a chemical mockery of spring. My landslide mind scrambles for that perfume, the ghost of an anonymous laundromat, a hide-away from his cigarettes and day-after beer sweat. With the groan of gears, something small inside me rattles loose. It makes a broken sound in the silence.

I force my breath even, write promises in the window's condensation. Next time. There will be a next time. Next time this road curves back into a shadow, my heart muscle contracts, his apology will spit glistening to slide with other fast-food containers on the rusting truck floor.

Next time.

The occasional moon shrugs, looks at her watch, and sighs.

Inquisition

How are you?
How do you do?
How do you do that?
How do you do
anything?

How do you place one foot in front of the other?
One breath after the next?
How does food taste on your tongue?
What explodes behind your closed eyes?
What does your mouth hold as you rock
jagged, weary on the 27 Bryant?

What came to you last night?
Who visited your dreams?
Who stretched thin as bile to shake the marrow of your bones?
Which are the moments that pull you towards death?
Which ones make you give yourself away?
Which of your heart beats tears the small green leaves
off cuttings of grief?

Which sobs are you fully committed to?
Which ones are an afterthought?
What crumbs did you leave as a path in the snowy woods?

What do you offer the wind,
when you beg to roll away in her furious hymn?
What is the angle between your chin and the hollow
of your throat as you walk away from me?

If we look in each other's eyes
will we see a way through?

Sideways

The world slumps sideways and I grab
his voice like the back of the bus seat.
As if my heart can be stilled by attending
to restrained, precise words. He is professional.
Allows a moment for his news to settle
to sink into my stalled mind.
He restarts a dispassionate description
of actions, situations, failed plans,
secrets guarded like love letters.

Present time falls back, memories
emerge from my thickened thoughts like
debris from a wave-ruined picnic. Soggy,
sand filled, itchy as they dry. The words
from our last conversation feel pointless
and precious, all the same.
The relative merits of vegetarian lasagna,
and under what circumstances jeans can
be appropriate for an engagement party.
Already sink below our horizon.

I wish I could have read the inscription
carved in the silence of her private loneliness.
Tried the handle when she seemed rigid
locked in our common bleakness.
Plans can change, be delayed. Oblivion
can snag, catch and unravel on any stray
hope. I shift my loss from hand
to hand, not yet able to hold that this time
her quiet had packed for a long journey
nothing more bearable than anything else.

The Salt of Ourselves

The moon pulls you away.
                                        her song still peals my breath.

The deltas beside my eyes brim with the salt of 16 years in this undertow.

Starlight flirts with the tense surface of the water.

        affectionate
                      mercurial

Withdrawing at the dim implication of a cloud
                                          wistful brevity of night.

Cool dark recedes giving way to a crimson dawn.

In that sanguine glow you drift
                    embracing the wind with every possible certainty.

My hands empty.   Dry like
summer sidewalk.

        Thoughts tangled weeds.

You   spread   in   all   directions

        Fearless   Glittering

        Expose a pearl hollow of enigmatic depth

Your ears hunger for promises
                                    secrets that shift like the sand

        or withstand the wrath of a season of storms.

I could hold the rain back more easily

                                    than I could keep you
                                              here.

Still in a calm
                                              you will
stagnate
                   evaporate
                         to a salt of yourself.

So, I balance
                         sift our confusion of sea and time.

Search the horizon for your fortune
                              accept the rhythm of waves.

Conspirators
    for my daughter, Zoe

I wade into melted twilight
my mind offers a souvenir.
Time crimps in memories' pull.

I lift your sleepy weight
sweat damp, bread warm.

Scoop you up, rock-back, knees bend shift
dance of the everyday and
your determined sleep.

I pull you into my chest
an ocean wave into shore
for the briefest
deepest of seconds
both of us sigh.

A syncopated hymn
release from the snaky tangle
of your car seat
of the growl and snipe of traffic.

I glance beyond
sticky lunch boxes
dirty sneakers
abandoned sweaters
flotsam of early weekday evenings.

There
like clouds parting.
Your secret smile.

A Creek Song
For Temescal in Ohlone Land

In a maze of shell
through illness and forgetting
around the hooves of horses and cattle
into the eager roots of seedlings
between the toes of someone's first stumble-steps
from oaky fingers of hills to rock in arms of the sea
people gather here.

Light dances
skims the surface
drops under patient shadows
then rises in a wink of sun.

Listen.

A melody of weaving
soars through luminous giggles
the snap and sigh of wet toes
tangled whispers of green.

The grace in the swish of a fluffy tail
curve of a bow stem, the spread leaves
a reverie broken by
staccato bark, chiding caw, a tired wail
all slip through this loamy
brown palm of earth
whose lifeline echoes a pulse of home.

The Day After

remember how after the fire
we held hands under the table
dreamed the same dream when we slept
I talked to your mother
for the very first time
she made French toast
generously
lent me
socks.

Bean
> *For my daughter, Iris*

we are steeped in quiet
folded in sheets and blankets
and you, small bean, so complete in sleep
your pink hat pulled to meet
downey eyebrows

breathe in the even light of dawn

our first morning is outside
today the world is broken open
every cell sings

Winter Nest

patient
unconcerned
hums along with growling morning traffic
her time is a different animal
wholly other from distracted human clutch

she watches milky clouds stretch tendrils across shallow daybreak
sympathetic and satisfied with their expanse
she gives her hours in gratitude to borrowed bones, the possibilities of being

potent as a cupped palm
she wears the softest shades, woven from shadows of dream-filled earth
when moved she chants in harmony with mourning doves
a dedication to the wisdom
tenacity of thorns

her incantations float akimbo, heedless to the confidence of gravity
their echo an embrace
her anchor as she delves into solitude

she understands her search, can predict her missteps
she has spent years reimagining what is leftover
discovers again the value in what she has always had

her core is burnished from this cycling
all the coming and going
all the offering and accommodation
this is what she celebrates perched
in petulant wind

This is her gift from the proprietor of clarity
Vision beyond our brash mechanistic borders
She is patient
as she waits for a season
to dream herself

Gravity's Daughter

Each night, she walks bed-less
a smoke-tinged exhalation
seeking asylum in the barren home of the street.

She swings her lantern
flings hope over warning
contradiction echoes
in her parched smile.
Her trail, a tranquil ruin through the waxy night.

This small woman
face closed as a fist
mind open as a precipice.
When she cracks
it sounds like breaking bone.

Haphazard
he approaches
into her silence.

An interruption that tears her wander.
His gaze sharp, vacant,
a predatory relic in apathetic streetlight.

His words melt in her ears
confusion of righteousness and privilege.
His proposition a mirage
catalogue of lies
squirm from his tongue
until he too is lost, adrift in his illusion.

But—she tears the caul
sloughing off his offering
the reasons he carefully salted
the itch in his phantom limb.

Her blood hears a song blown from the lips of fall's fury.
A rhythm rejoicing, gathering effervescence under her skin.

The Rusalki come unstrung.
Each mistress of her own precise grief.
Vengeful sirens
every girl's friend
they swim too close to the bones
of this wounded suckling world.
They cut their teeth on aborted promises
writhe in the blood, whistle through tears.
drive the waves in singular sorority.

They beat their wings till it's all undone –
this sleep in search of a flying dream.
She's vaulted on their voices
soars through flinty laughter
deaf to his calls, immune to generic time.
She is gravity's daughter
apprentice to catastrophe.

His alibi slides from her shoulders.
Her hips shake freedom from chipped bits of bone.
Her arms unfurl among immaculate stars.
Her feet break free of remorse—
leaves the sidewalk empty handed
as she communes with their storm.

Sara **Biel** is a poet, visual artist and social worker living in Oakland, CA. She is coeditor of the Colossus Press anthology series. Sara has had poems published in *sparkle and blink; Button Eye Review, Beyond Words Literary Magazine* and won honorable mention in the *Streetlight* magazine 2021 poetry contest. Her work has been included in *Our Spirits Cary our Voices* and *Words Upon the Waters*. She is interested in creative process as a medium for change, healing and building community.

www.ingramcontent.com/pod-product-compliance
Lightning Source LLC
Chambersburg PA
CBHW022124090426
42743CB00008B/1001